CONTENTS

MATERIALS

yarn

darning needle

Yarn
Commonly spun from wool or acrylic fibres, yarn comes in many colours and thicknesses. Most projects are made in standard double knitting (DK) yarn or in thicker, chunky yarn.

Knitting needles
Different sizes, or thicknesses, of needles are used for different types of yarn. In this book you will be using 3.25 mm, 4 mm and 6.5 mm needles.

Darning needle
A thick needle with a large eye and blunt point, used for sewing yarn.

Sewing needle and thread
A thin needle and fine thread, best for sewing on buttons and fasteners.

Felt
This thick cloth is great for adding details to knitted projects.

Air erasable fabric pen
The ink in this pen becomes invisible over 24 hours so it is great for marking on felt. You could also use tailor's chalk.

Crochet hook
A short, hooked tool, useful for hooking yarn through gaps in knitting.

knitting needles

TECHNIQUES

Garter stitch
Knit every row (see page 6). Both sides will look the same.

Stocking stitch
Knit a row, then purl a row (see page 6). The front will have rows of 'v' stitches, the back will look like garter stitch.

Changing yarn colour
On a new row, tie the tail of the new yarn to the end of the old yarn and start knitting with the new colour.

Darning in loose ends
Sew in loose yarn by taking the needle through a few stitches at the back of the fabric.

craft Smart

KNITTING

Adel Kay

QED

QED Publishing

QED Project Editor: Ruth Symons

Created for QED Publishing by Tall Tree Ltd
Editor: Catherine Saunders
Designers: Jonathan Vipond and Marisa Renzullo
Illustrator: Barry Croucher
Photography: Michael Wicks

Copyright © QED Publishing 2013

First published in the UK in 2013 by
QED Publishing, a Quarto Group company
230 City Road
London EC1V 2TT
www.qed-publishing.co.uk

A catalogue record for this book is available from the British Library.

ISBN 978 1 78171 096 8

Printed in China

Picture credits
(t=top, b=bottom, l=left, r=right, c=centre, fc=front cover, bc=back cover)
Shutterstock Andrey Armyagov, fcc; Annto, fcc, bcc; CLM, 4tl; Crepesoles, fcc, bct 3bc, 4r, 16r; Garsya, fc, bcc; IDAL, 3tl, 12c; Iryna1, 3r, 29r; Ivancovlad, 261; Iwona Grodzka, fcr, bcl; kuma, 3t, tr; kzww, 3br, 4tr; Madlen, 3r, 12t, 26r; mholka, fcc, bct; Nattika, fcbr; oksana2010, bctl; OlyaSenko, 4–32 bl/br; Picsfive, bctr, 3bl, 14c; s73, 6, 9, 11, 13, 15, 16, 21, 23, 25, 27, 29, 31; Sergey Mironov, 3l; Thomas Klee, 3bc, 22r; victoriaKh, 3rc, 14rc; Vodoleyka, 20r, 24r; Vysokova Ekaterina, 3r, 16c.

Note to Adults:
Some children might be able to do some or all of these projects on their own, while others might need more help. These are projects that you can work on together, not only to avoid any problems or accidents, but also to share in the fun of making crafts.

In preparation of this book, all due care has been exercised with regard to the activities and advice depicted. The publishers regret that they can accept no liability for any loss or injury sustained.

At the top of the page for each project you will find this handy key. It will tell you the difficulty level to expect from each project:

Quick creative fix
These projects are quick, easy and perfect for a beginner.

Sharpen your skills
Confident with your beginner skills? Move onto these slightly tougher projects.

Ready for a challenge
For a challenging project you can really get stuck into.

Creative masterpiece
Think you can tackle the toughest knitting projects? Have a go at these.

CASTING ON

1 Make a loop of yarn. Pull another loop through it and place it onto a needle. Pull tighter.

2 Insert the tip of the right needle through the front of the loop and under the needle.

3 Wind the yarn under and over the point of the right needle.

4 Use the right needle to draw the yarn through the stitch and create a loop.

5 Insert the left needle into the back of the loop to make a second stitch.

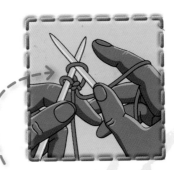

6 Repeat steps 2 to 5 until you have the required number of stitches.

CASTING OFF

1 Knit two stitches. Insert the left needle into the first stitch knitted. Lift it and pull it over the second stitch.

2 Knit the next stitch. Lift the first stitch over the second. Repeat this until one stitch is left on your right needle. Cut the yarn and pull the tail through the last stitch.

KNIT STITCH

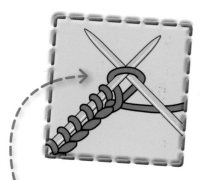

1 Insert the point of the right needle into the front of the first stitch from front to back.

2 Wind the yarn under and over the point of the right needle.

3 Use the right needle to pull the yarn through the stitch to create a loop. Slip the stitch off the left needle.

PURL STITCH

1 Hold the needle with stitches in your left hand. Insert the point of your right needle into the first stitch, from back to front.

2 Wind the yarn around the right needle tip from right to left.

3 Use your right needle to pull the yarn back through the stitch to create a loop.

4 Slip the stitch off the left needle. You now have one purl stitch made on your right needle.

KNIT 2 TOGETHER
This is just like a knit stitch. Insert your right needle into two stitches. Wrap the yarn around the needle as normal, pull it through, then slip both stitches off your left needle.

6

SEWING TECHNIQUES

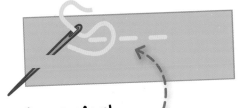

Running stitch

Sew up and down through the fabric. Make sure the stitches on both the topside and underside are the same size and in a straight line.

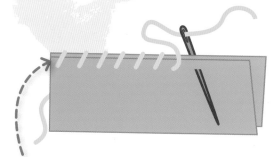

Over stitch

Place the two edges of the fabric you are joining close together. Sew stitches from one piece of fabric to the other to bind them tightly.

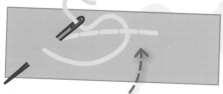

Back stitch

Make a running stitch, then come up through the fabric a stitch ahead. Stitch backwards to meet your first running stitch. Repeat in a neat line.

KNITTING A TENSION SQUARE

Some patterns in this book suggest you knit a tension square first. This helps you to check that your knitting will come out at the right size.

Knit a square slightly larger than 10 x 10 cm. Follow the tension square pattern, then count how many 'v' stitches there are horizontally and how many 'v' rows there are vertically in a 10 x 10 cm area. This will give you your 'tension gauge', eg 24 stitches x 30 rows.

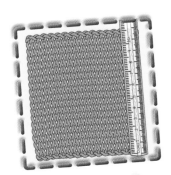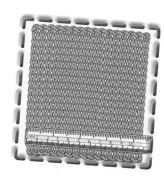

If you have more stitches and rows in your square than there are in the 'pattern gauge', change to larger needles. If you have fewer stitches and rows change to smaller needles.

FLOWER PURSE

Use star stitch to decorate this handy knitted purse.

 START HERE

Knitting pattern

FINISHED ITEM LAID FLAT MEASURES: 10 × 8 cm

BEGIN: Cast on 24 stitches in red yarn.

NEXT: Knit every row until your work measures 20 cm.

END: Cast off.

STAR STITCH

Pull your needle up through at point 1 and re-insert your needle at point 2. Pull up your needle at point 3 and re-insert at point 4, and so on.

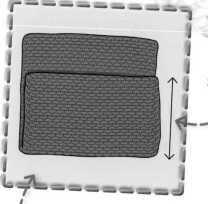

8.5 cm

1 Measure 8.5 cm from the cast off edge and fold the fabric over to make the body of the purse.

2 Fold over the top flap. Use a darning needle and the yellow yarn to sew the large button in the centre.

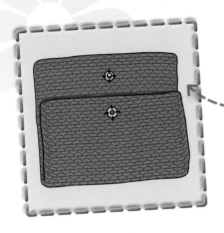

3 Using the sewing thread, sew the top of the snap fastener onto the underside of the flap, under the button. Sew the bottom of the snap fastener onto the body of the purse so that it lines up with the top fastener.

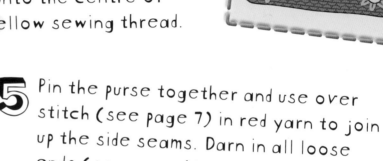

4 Use double-threaded yarn and star stitch to sew one large star and two smaller ones onto the front of the purse. Sew the small buttons onto the centre of each star, using yellow sewing thread.

5 Pin the purse together and use over stitch (see page 7) in red yarn to join up the side seams. Darn in all loose ends (see page 4) and remove the pins.

This purse makes a great gift and can be knitted in any colour you like!

9

PHONE CASE

Keep your phone safe and stylish with a cosy cover.

 START HERE

Knitting pattern

FINISHED ITEM LAID FLAT MEASURES:
8 x 12 cm

PHONE CASE:

BEGIN: Cast on 19 stitches in blue yarn.

NEXT: Knit every row until your work measures 20 cm (garter stitch, see page 4).

END: Cast off.

STRAP (OPTIONAL):

BEGIN: Cast on 4 stitches in blue.

NEXT: Knit every row until strap measures 20 cm.

END: Cast off.

LAZY DAISY

Come up through the fabric and make a small loop. Then push the needle down next to where it came up. Come up again inside the top of the loop, and make a small stitch to hold it in place. Repeat for each petal.

13 cm

1 Measure 13 cm from the cast off edge and fold the fabric up. Fold over the top flap and sew the yellow button in the centre, using the darning needle.

2 Sew the top of the snap fastener onto the underside of the flap, under the button. Sew the bottom of the snap fastener below the flap. Make sure that it lines up with the top fastener.

3 Use white yarn to embroider flower petals on the top flap using lazy daisy stitch.

4 Pin the case together and stitch up the side seams using over stitch (see page 7) and the blue yarn. Remove the pins.

5 Pin each end of the strap to the sides of the phone case. Sew on using over stitch and blue yarn to finish. Darn in all loose ends and remove the pins.

You could sew a felt or fabric shape onto your phone case instead of embroidering it. Sew on any extra details, such as eyes.

CORSAGE BROOCH

Jazz up your outfit with this knitted brooch. You can knit it in one or two colours.

Knitting pattern

FINISHED ITEM MEASURES: 5 × 5 cm

TWO COLOUR BROOCH:

BEGIN: Cast on 60 stitches in yarn A.
Cut the yarn 30 cm from the needle.

NEXT: Join with yarn B (see page 4). Knit 5 rows.

ROW 6: Knit 2 together (see page 6). Repeat this until the end of the row. (30 stitches left.)

ROW 7: Work the same as the previous row. (15 stitches left.)

END: Cast off. Leave 60 cm of yarn for sewing up.

To knit a single colour brooch follow the same pattern but do not cut the yarn or add a new yarn.

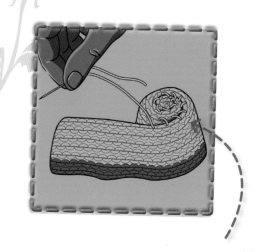

1 Thread the tail of yarn B onto the darning needle. With the cast off edge face up, roll the fabric. As you roll, darn the fabric together along the edge, using over stitch (see page 7). Darn in the end. Turn the piece over and thread the tail of yarn A through to the back of the corsage.

2 Draw a leaf shape on the paper. Use it as a template to cut out two felt leaves. Draw veins onto the leaves, using the fabric pen or chalk.

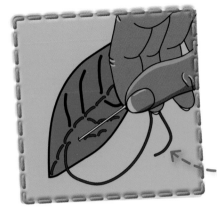

3 Split the embroidery thread so that you have two sets of three strands. Darn the veins onto the leaves using back stitch (see page 7).

4 Sew the leaves onto the back of the flower, using over stitch and embroidery thread.

5 Use the loose yarn from step 1 and over stitch to attach a brooch back. Darn in the loose ends.

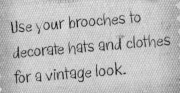
Use your brooches to decorate hats and clothes for a vintage look.

SUGAR PLUM CUSHION

This mini cushion is easy to knit and makes a cute present.

Knitting pattern

TENSION SQUARE PATTERN:

Knit a tension square (see page 7) by casting on 18 stitches and knitting 24 rows in stocking stitch (see page 4).

Pattern gauge: 14 stitches × 19 rows

FINISHED ITEM LAID FLAT MEASURES:
25.5 × 25.5 cm

CUSHION:

BEGIN: Cast on 36 stitches in pink yarn.

NEXT: Work stocking stitch (see page 4) until your work measures 74 cm.

END: Cast off.

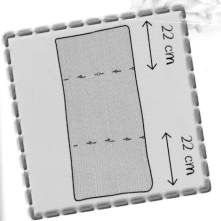

22 cm

22 cm

1 Insert two lines of pins 22 cm from the top and bottom edges of the fabric. This marks out the square on the front where you will embroider the flowers.

2 Draw an 8 × 8 cm flower on some paper and cut it out. Use this as a template to cut three flowers out of felt.

3 Pin the flowers onto the top of the fabric. Using DK yarn and a darning needle, sew a button over each flower and through the back of the fabric. Remove the pins from the felt.

4 Embroider stems and leaves for each flower using lime green chunky yarn and back stitch (see page 7). Remove the two lines of pins.

5 Fold the top back 22 cm so that the front is on the inside. Pin and sew up the side seams using over stitch (see page 7). Repeat this with the bottom section. Remove the pins and darn in the loose ends. Turn the cushion right side out and insert the pad.

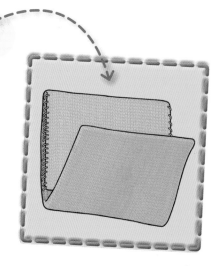

Use your felt and yarn to create any shape or design. How about some fish in an ocean scene or just a crazy pattern?

BEADED SCARF

Accessorize a simple knitted scarf with beads and tassels.

YOU WILL NEED:
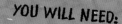

- 2 × 100 g/137 m balls turquoise chunky yarn (that uses 6.5 mm needles)
- A 100 g/137 m ball of lime green chunky yarn
- 6.5 mm knitting needles
- 6.5 mm crochet hook
- Darning needle
- Assorted beads (with a wide hole)
- Tape measure
- Scissors

START HERE

Knitting pattern

TENSION SQUARE PATTERN:

Knit a tension square (see page 7) by casting on 16 stitches and knitting 25 rows in garter stitch (see page 4).

Pattern gauge: 12 stitches × 21 rows

FINISHED ITEM LAID FLAT MEASURES:
16 × 150 cm (excluding tassels)

BEADED SCARF:

BEGIN: Cast on 20 stitches in turquoise yarn.

NEXT: Work garter stitch (see page 4) until your work measures 150 cm.

END: Cast off.
Darn in all loose ends.

Use the pattern on page 18 to make a matching hat.

1 Cut 38 pieces of lime green yarn, each 70 cm long. Hold two lengths of yarn and loop them in half. Use the crochet hook to pull the loop between the first and second 'v' knit stitches on the scarf.

2 Thread the yarn ends through the loop you just made and pull firmly to secure.

3 Do this for the remaining **18** spaces. Repeat steps **1** to **3** on the other end of the scarf.

4 Make a knot in the tassel and use the darning needle to thread on a bead. Knot the yarn under the bead to keep it in place.

5 Add as many beads as you want and then trim all the tassels to the same length.

Add a different colour yarn (see page 4) to make a striped scarf in the colours of your favourite sports team.

BEAR HAT

You'll never want to leave home without this furry friend.

YOU WILL NEED:

- A 100 g/137 m ball of beige chunky yarn (that uses 6.5 mm knitting needles)
- A 100 g/137 m ball of brown chunky yarn
- A small quantity of black DK yarn
- A small quantity of white DK yarn
- 6.5 mm knitting needles
- White sewing thread
- Black sewing thread
- Darning needle
- Round end pins
- Tape measure
- Black and white felt
- Cardboard
- Paper, pencil and scissors

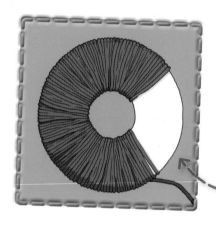

1 Cut two identical 4.5 cm cardboard rings. Wrap the brown yarn around the ring until the hole in the middle is very tight.

2 Cut the yarn along the edge, between the cardboard rings. Pass a length of yarn between the cardboard rings and tie it tightly. Remove the cardboard. Make another ear in the same way and sew both onto the hat.

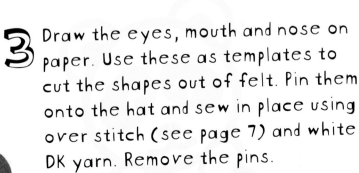

3 Draw the eyes, mouth and nose on paper. Use these as templates to cut the shapes out of felt. Pin them onto the hat and sew in place using over stitch (see page 7) and white DK yarn. Remove the pins.

Knitting pattern

TENSION SQUARE PATTERN:

Knit a tension square (see page 7) by casting on 18 stitches and knitting 24 rows in stocking stitch (see page 4).

Pattern gauge: 14 stitches x 19 rows

FINISHED ITEM WILL FIT:

53 cm head circumference

ANIMAL HAT:

BEGIN: Cast on 66 stitches in beige yarn.

ROW 1: Knit 2 stitches, purl 2 stitches and repeat this to the end of the row. Knit 2 stitches.

ROW 2: Purl 2 stitches, knit 2 stitches and repeat until the end of the row. Purl 2 stitches.

ROWS 3 and 4: Work as rows 1 and 2.

NEXT: Work 16 rows or 9 cm in stocking stitch ending on a purl row. If you want a longer hat add more rows in multiples of two.

DECREASING:

ROW 1: Knit 6 stitches, knit 2 together (see page 6). Repeat 8 times. Knit 2 stitches. (58 stitches left.)

ROW 2: Purl this row and every following even row (4, 6, 8, 10, 12, 14).

ROW 3: Knit 5 stitches, knit 2 together. Repeat 8 times. Knit 2 stitches. (50 stitches left.)

ROW 5: Knit 4 stitches, knit 2 together. Repeat 8 times. Knit 2 stitches. (42 stitches left.)

ROW 7: Knit 3 stitches, knit 2 together. Repeat 8 times. Knit 2 stitches. (34 stitches left.)

ROW 9: Knit 2 stitches, knit 2 together. Repeat 8 times. Knit 2 stitches. (26 stitches left.)

ROW 11: Knit 1 stitch, knit 2 together. Repeat 8 times. Knit 2 stitches. (18 stitches left.)

ROW 13: Knit 2 together. Repeat this until the end of the row. (9 stitches left.)

END: Cut the yarn approximately 30 cm from the needle. Thread the tail onto a darning needle and pass each stitch from your knitting needle to the darning needle. Then pull the yarn through firmly and darn in the loose end (see page 4).

4 Embroider a couple of white over stitches onto each eye. Embroider the mouth features in black DK yarn, using back stitch (see page 7).

EGG COSY

A bunny egg cosy looks as cute as can be on your breakfast table!

YOU WILL NEED:

- A small quantity of pale blue 4 ply yarn (that uses 3.25 mm knitting needles)
- Small quantities of black and pink DK yarn
- 3.25 mm knitting needles
- Darning needle
- Tape measure
- Round end pins
- Scissors

1 Turn the cosy inside out. Sew the seam using over stitch (see page 7). Darn in the loose ends.

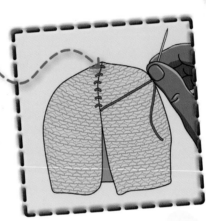

2 Turn the cosy right side out so the seam is at the back. Pinch the straight edges of the ears together and pin them onto the egg cosy. Use the yarn tail to darn them in place.

3 Use black yarn to embroider two over stitches for each eye and three back stitches for the mouth (see page 7). Embroider two back stitches in pink yarn for the nose.

20

Knitting pattern

FINISHED ITEM LAID FLAT MEASURES:
6 x 10 cm (including the ears)

EGG COSY:

BEGIN: Cast on 42 stitches in pale blue yarn.

NEXT: Work stocking stitch (see page 4) for 20 rows.

DECREASING:

ROW 21: Knit 1 stitch, knit 2 together. Repeat this until the end of the row.
(28 stitches left.)

ROW 22: Purl this row.

ROW 23: Knit 2 together. Repeat this until the end of the row. (14 stitches left.)

ROW 24: Purl this row.

END: Draw the yarn through the stitches (see page 19).

EARS (MAKE TWO)

BEGIN: Cast on 10 stitches in pale blue yarn.

NEXT: Work stocking stitch for 12 rows.

ROW 13: Knit 1 stitch, knit 2 together. Knit 4 stitches, knit 2 together. Knit 1 stitch.
(8 stitches left.)

ROW 14: Purl this row and every following even row (16, 18).

ROW 15: Knit 1 stitch, knit 2 together. Knit 2 stitches, knit 2 together. Knit 1 stitch.
(6 stitches left.)

ROW 17: Knit 1 stitch, knit 2 together twice. Knit 1 stitch. (4 stitches left.)

ROW 19: Knit 2 together twice.
(2 stitches left.)

END: Draw the yarn through the stitches.

Make a chick using yellow yarn. Cut out a beak and two wings in yellow felt and sew onto the cosy using yellow thread.

MUG WARMER

Keep your drink hot with a personalized knitted mug warmer.

YOU WILL NEED:

- A small quantity of pale pink DK yarn
- A small quantity of cream DK yarn
- 4 mm knitting needles
- Darning needle
- Round end pins
- Mug
- Red felt
- Tape measure
- Ruler
- Pencil, paper and scissors

Knitting pattern

FINISHED ITEM LAID FLAT MEASURES:
26 x 9 cm (to fit a standard 26 x 10 cm mug)

BEGIN: Cast on 58 stitches in pale pink yarn.

ROW 1: Knit 1 stitch, purl 1 stitch.
Repeat this until the end of the row.

NEXT: Repeat row 1 until your work measures 9 cm.

END: Cast off.

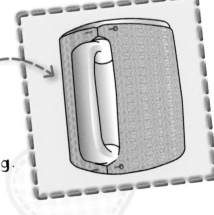

1 Pin the fabric together at the top and bottom, leaving the middle of the seam open. Place around the mug.

2 Draw a heart on the paper, about 7 x 6 cm. Cut it out and pin it onto the red felt.

3 Cut out the heart from the felt and pin it onto the cosy.

4 Carefully remove the fabric from the mug. Using cream DK yarn, stitch the heart onto the warmer with running stitch (see page 7). Remove the pins.

5 Turn the cosy inside out and re-pin the top and bottom seams. Sew a 1cm seam at the top and bottom using over stitch (see page 7). Darn in the loose ends. Turn the cosy right side out.

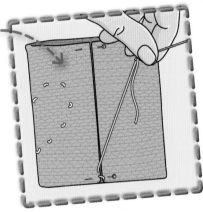

You can use felt to create any design. How about a butterfly or a star? Or even the first letter of your name?

MINI HANDBAG

Complete your outfit with a stylish mini handbag.

YOU WILL NEED:

- A 100 g/280 m ball of lilac DK yarn
- A 50 g/140 m ball of blue DK yarn
- 4 mm knitting needles
- Button
- Purple felt
- Darning needle
- Round end pins
- Tape measure
- Pencil, paper and scissors

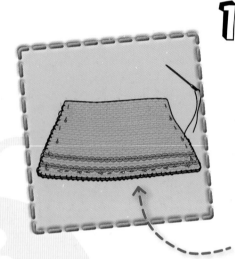

1 With the right sides facing inwards, pin the seams of the two bag pieces together. Sew the bottom and side seams up using over stitch (see page 7). Remove the pins and turn the bag right side out.

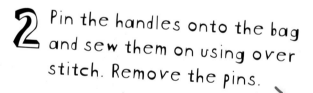

2 Pin the handles onto the bag and sew them on using over stitch. Remove the pins.

3 On paper, draw a flower about 8 x 8 cm. Use this as a template to cut a flower out of felt. Pin the flower onto the bag. Sew the button onto the felt flower and the bag. Remove the pins.

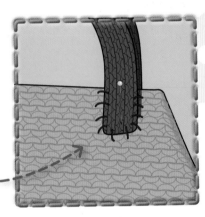

START HERE

Knitting pattern

FINISHED ITEM LAID FLAT MEASURES:
22 x 23 cm (excluding the handles)

BAG SIDES (MAKE TWO):

BEGIN: Cast on 44 stitches in lilac yarn.

ROWS 1 TO 6: Work garter stitch (see page 4) for 6 rows.

DECREASING:
ROW 7: (Right side) Join with blue yarn. Knit 2 stitches, knit 2 together. Knit to last 4 stitches, knit 2 together, knit 2 stitches. (42 stitches left.)

ROW 8: Knit this row. Cut the yarn 30 cm from the needle.

ROWS 9 TO 12: Join with lilac yarn and knit 5 rows.

ROWS 13 AND 14: Work as rows 7 and 8. (40 stitches left.)

ROWS 15 TO 18: Work as rows 9 to 12.

ROW 19: Knit 2 stitches, knit 2 together. Knit to last 4 stitches, knit 2 together, knit 2 stitches. (38 stitches left.)

ROWS 20 TO 24: Knit 5 rows.

ROWS 25 TO 30: Work as rows 19 to 24. (36 stitches left.)

ROWS 31 TO 36: Work as rows 19 to 24. (34 stitches left.)

ROWS 37 TO 42: Work as rows 19 to 24. (32 stitches left.)

END: Cast off.

HANDLES (MAKE TWO):

BEGIN: Cast on 7 stitches in blue yarn.

ROW 1: Knit a stitch, purl a stitch. Repeat to the end of the row, ending with a knit stitch.

NEXT: Work as row 1 until your work measures about 32 cm.

END: Cast off.

Leave out the handles to turn your handbag into a stylish clutch bag. Sew snap fasteners onto the inside of the bag and cover these stitches with a button, bead or felt.

25

HAND WARMERS

Keep your wrists and hands warm with these toasty fingerless gloves.

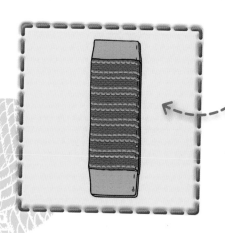

1 Take one knitted piece and fold it over so that the right side is facing inwards. Pin along the seam. Repeat with the other piece.

2 On the first piece, darn a 5 cm top seam, using over stitch (see page 7). Darn in the end. Leave 5 cm of the seam open for the thumb hole. Darn a 10 cm bottom seam using over stitch. Repeat on the second piece.

5 cm

10 cm

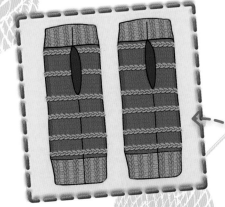

3 Remove the pins from both pieces. Darn in the loose ends and turn the hand warmers right side out.

Knitting pattern

TENSION SQUARE PATTERN:

Knit a tension square (see page 7) by casting on 26 stitches and knitting 32 rows in stocking stitch (see page 4).
Pattern gauge: 22 stitches × 28 rows

FINISHED ITEM LAID FLAT MEASURES:

9 × 20 cm (or 10 × 20 cm)

HAND WARMER (MAKE TWO):

Begin: Cast on 38 stitches (42 for bigger hands) in pale pink yarn.

RIB:

ROW 1: Knit 2 stitches, purl 2 stitches. Repeat this until the end of the row.

ROW 2: Purl 2 stitches, knit 2 stitches. Repeat this until the end of the row.

ROWS 3 TO 10: Work as rows 1 and 2, four times.

ROWS 11 AND 12: Knit 2 rows. Cut the yarn, leaving a 30 cm length for sewing up.

MAIN PATTERN:

ROWS 13 TO 16: Join with the turquoise yarn (see page 4) and work 4 rows in stocking stitch. Do not cut the yarn.

ROWS 17 AND 18: Join with the pale pink yarn and knit 2 rows. Cut the yarn leaving a 30 cm length for sewing up.

PATTERN REPEAT:

ROWS 19 TO 22: Pick up turquoise yarn and work 4 rows in stocking stitch. Do not cut the yarn.

ROWS 23 AND 24: Join with pink yarn and knit 2 rows. Cut the yarn, leaving a 30 cm length for sewing up.

ROWS 25 TO 54. Repeat rows 19 to 24 five times. Do not cut the yarn on row 54.

RIB:

Work as rows 1 and 2 (three times). (60 rows worked.)

END: Cast off.

Hand warmers are a great idea if you have cold hands but still need to use your fingers!

HEADBAND

This stylish headband looks great and keeps your ears warm!

START HERE

YOU WILL NEED:

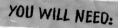

- A 100 g/280 m ball of blue DK yarn (that uses 4 mm knitting needles)
- A small quantity of white DK yarn
- 4 mm knitting needles
- Darning needle
- Round end pins
- Turquoise felt
- Button
- 1.5 m of thin ribbon
- Tape measure
- Pencil, paper and scissors

Knitting pattern

TENSION SQUARE PATTERN:

Knit a tension square (see page 7) by casting on 16 stitches and knitting 25 rows in stocking stitch (see page 4).
Pattern gauge: 22 stitches × 28 rows

FINISHED ITEM SIZE:

Measure around your head and knit a piece 2 cm shorter than your measurement. It will be roughly 53 cm.

HEADBAND:

BEGIN: Cast on 22 stitches in blue yarn.

ROW 1: Knit this row. (This will be the right side.)

ROW 2: Knit 3 stitches, purl 16 stitches, knit 3 stitches.

NEXT: Repeat rows 1 and 2 until your work is the length you need.

END: Cast off. Cut the yarn, leaving approximately 50 cm for sewing up the seam.

1 Fold over the fabric so that the right side is inside and pin along the side seam.

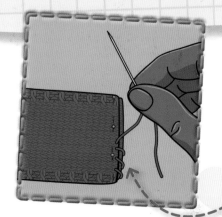

2 Sew the seam up using over stitch (see page 7). Darn in the loose ends. Remove the pins. Turn the fabric right side out.

3 Thread the ribbon onto the darning needle. Starting at the seam, sew the ribbon around the headband, using running stitch (see page 7). Make sure you sew the ribbon inside the textured edge.

4 Put the headband on and tie the ribbon ends together in a bow. Remove the headband.

5 On paper, draw a flower about 8 x 8 cm. Use it as a template to cut the same shape out of the felt. Pin the flower onto the headband. Sew the button onto the felt flower and the headband. Remove the pins and darn in the loose ends.

This headband looks great in any colour. A different-coloured felt flower also looks stylish.

SQUISHY PENGUIN

This huggable penguin would look great perched by your bed!

YOU WILL NEED:

- A small quantity of cream DK yarn
- A small quantity of black DK yarn
- 3.25 mm knitting needles
- Yellow and white felt
- Yellow sewing thread
- Toy stuffing
- Darning needle
- Round end pins
- Tape measure
- Pencil, paper and scissors

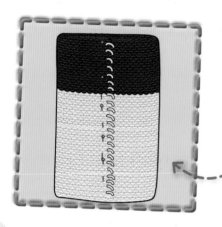

1 Fold the fabric over with the right side facing inwards. This will make a seam in the centre. Pin and sew up the seam using over stitch (see page 7). Remove the pins.

2 Sew running stitch (see page 7) around the cast off edge using the black yarn tail. Pull the yarn firmly to gather the fabric. Darn the edges and the yarn end in securely.

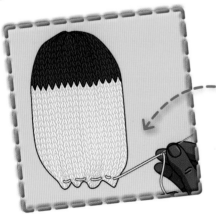

3 Turn the fabric right side out. Fill with toy stuffing. Repeat step 2 with the cream yarn.

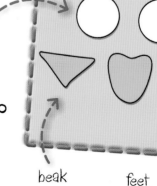

eyes

beak   feet

4 On paper, draw two circles for the eyes, a triangle for the beak and two feet. Use these as templates to cut the shapes out of felt.

Knitting pattern

FINISHED ITEM MEASURES:
8 × 13 cm

HEAD AND BODY:

BEGIN: Cast on 50 stitches in cream yarn. Work stocking stitch (see page 4) until the work measures 9 cm and ends in a purl row. Cut the yarn 30 cm from the needle.

NEXT: Join with black yarn. Work stocking stitch until the work measures 13 cm and ends in a purl row.

END: Cast off.

WINGS (MAKE TWO)

BEGIN: Cast on 9 stitches in black yarn.

ROWS 1–14: Work stocking stitch for 14 rows.

DECREASING:

ROW 15: Knit 1 stitch, knit 2 together, knit 3 stitches, knit 2 together, knit 1 stitch. (7 stitches left.)

ROW 16: Purl this row and all other even rows (18, 20).

ROW 17: Knit 1 stitch, knit 2 together, knit 1 stitch, knit 2 together, knit 1 stitch. (5 stitches left.)

ROW 19: Knit 2 together, knit 1 stitch, knit 2 together. (3 stitches left.)

ROW 21: Knit 2 together, knit 1 stitch. (2 stitches left.)

END: Draw the yarn through the stitches (see page 19).

5 Sew the felt eyes onto the penguin using two back stitches (see page 7). Sew the wings on using over stitch. Sew on the beak and feet, using over stitches on each side. Darn in the loose ends.

To make a square toy, like this owl, skip steps 2 and 3 and sew a seam along the cast off edge. Knot several yarn lengths together to make ears.

31

INDEX